Alfred's Basic Piano Library

Prep Course

FOR THE YOUNG BEGINNER

Willard A. Palmer • Morton Manus • Amanda Vick Lethco

Theory Book • Level F

INSTRUCTIONS FOR USE

1. This book is designed for use with Alfred's PREP COURSE for the YOUNG BEGINNER, LESSON BOOK F. The first assignment should be made when the student receives the Lesson Book.

2. As with all the supplementary books of this series, the pages of this THEORY BOOK are coordinated page by page with the LESSON BOOK. Assignments should be made according to the instructions in the upper right corner of each page in this THEORY BOOK. This ensures that each concept being taught in the Lesson Book receives more than adequate drill, while old principles are constantly and thoroughly reviewed.

3. After the opening MELODIC INTERVAL REVIEW and the exercise reinforcing the concept of BASSO OSTINATO, which is introduced on the corresponding pages of the Lesson Book, the student is given "in depth" drills in SYNCOPATED RHYTHM, a concept that is emphasized throughout Level F.

4. In this level the student is introduced to TRIADS for the first time. The authors have considered it very important to wait until the young beginner has had the opportunity to build the bridge of the hand by playing many harmonic intervals before three-note chords are attempted. In Level F, the primary chords of the keys of C, G and D major are introduced, and the many drills contained in this book will ensure that every student can instantly recognize and identify them, whether used as block or broken chords.

5. This book ends with a very thorough review of all concepts taught in the PREP COURSE. This is done with five exceptionally attractive and interesting pages, consisting of THE BIG PUZZLE, THE BIG QUIZ and SCRAMBLED PRIMARIES. The completion of these pages, along with the final pages of Lesson Book F, will usher the student into Alfred's BASIC PIANO LIBRARY, regular Level 3.

Illustrations by Christine Finn   •   Music Engraving by Nancy Butler   •   Layout by Tom Gerou

Melodic Interval Review
(Three-Way Match)

1. On the keyboards in the boxes in the left column, the shaded keys represent MELODIC INTERVALS (played one key at a time). Draw lines connecting the dots on these boxes to the dots on the boxes in the center column that have the correct interval names.

2. Draw lines connecting the dots on the boxes in the center column to the dots on the boxes in the right column that show the written intervals.

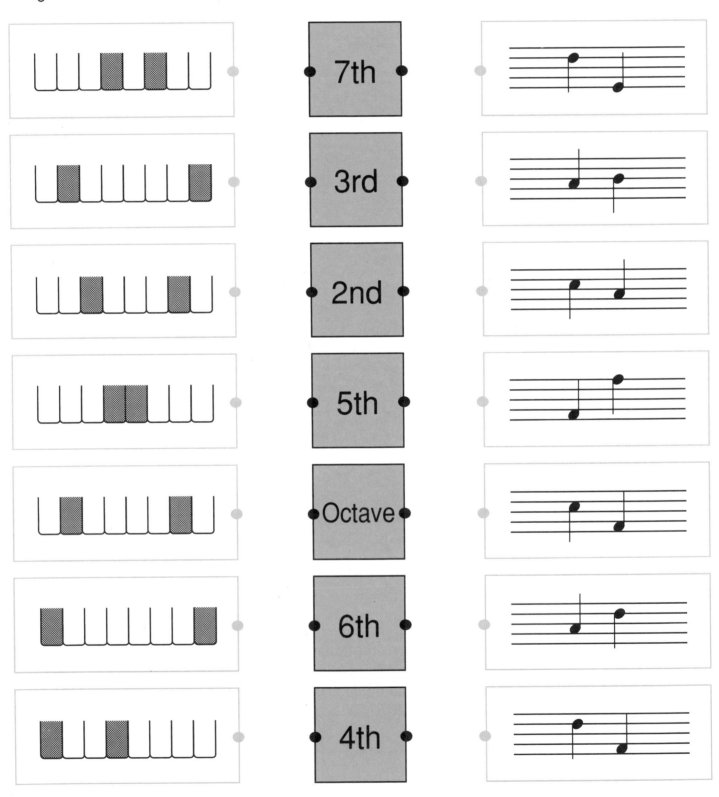

Score 10 for each pair of boxes correctly connected.

PERFECT SCORE = 140   YOUR SCORE _____

Add an Ostinato

When the same pattern of notes is played over and over
in the bass, it is called *BASSO OSTINATO,* or "obstinate bass."

The melody on this page works well with the
following two-measure pattern:

1. In the music below, write the above two-measure pattern over and over on the bass staffs.
    In the second ending you will be able to add only the first measure of the pattern.
    Be sure to align the bass notes so they are directly below the treble notes with which they are played.

2. Play the piece several times. Be sure to bring out the melody by playing it a little louder than the bass.

Adagio moderato

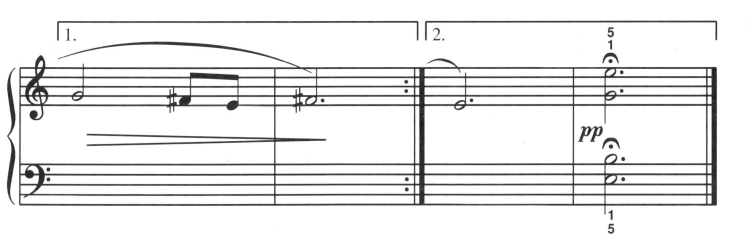

Syncopated Rap!

Use with pages 8–9.

Notes played between the main beats of the measure and held across the beat are called *SYNCOPATED NOTES.*

SYNCOPATED NOTE

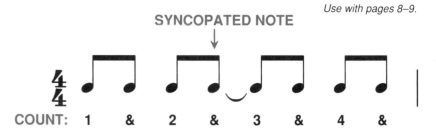

1. Say the words in rhythm while you clap your hands and tap your foot four times for each measure. Snap your fingers on each note shaped like an X. Rap all eighth notes EVENLY.
2. Circle all of the syncopated notes. (Include both tied notes in each circle.)

   How many syncopated notes are there? _____.

Andante moderato

Syncopated Song

Use with pages 8–9.

3. Now play the music that goes with the words of *SYNCOPATED RAP.*
   You may use the same words if you would like to sing this song.

Andante moderato

Triads

A TRIAD IS A THREE-NOTE CHORD.

THE THREE NOTES OF A TRIAD ARE:

Use with pages 10–11.

| ROOT 1 | THIRD 3 | FIFTH 5 |

5th
3rd
ROOT

OR

5th
3rd
ROOT

The ROOT is the note from which the triad gets its name. The ROOT of a C triad is C.

To build a triad, measure the 3rd and the 5th upward from the ROOT.
When a triad is in ROOT POSITION (with the root at the bottom),
all the notes of the triad will be on LINES, or *all* of them will be in SPACES.

1. Build triads using each of the following LINE NOTES as the root.

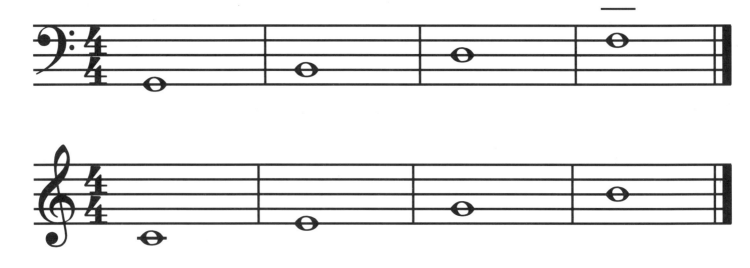

2. Build triads using each of the following SPACE NOTES as the root.

3. Play all of the above triads, using LH 5 3 1 or RH 1 3 5.
    Say "G triad, B triad," etc., as you play. The name of each triad is the same as the given ROOT.

Spelling Root Position Triads

This page prepares you for the very important TRIAD VOCABULARY introduced on
page 14 of the Lesson Book.

To spell the names of the notes of any triad in ROOT POSITION (with the ROOT on the BOTTOM),
you must always skip one letter of the musical alphabet between each of the three notes.
For example, the A TRIAD in root position is A C E. The G TRIAD is G B D, etc.

1. Write the names of the notes of each of the following triads in the boxes,
   as shown in the first example.

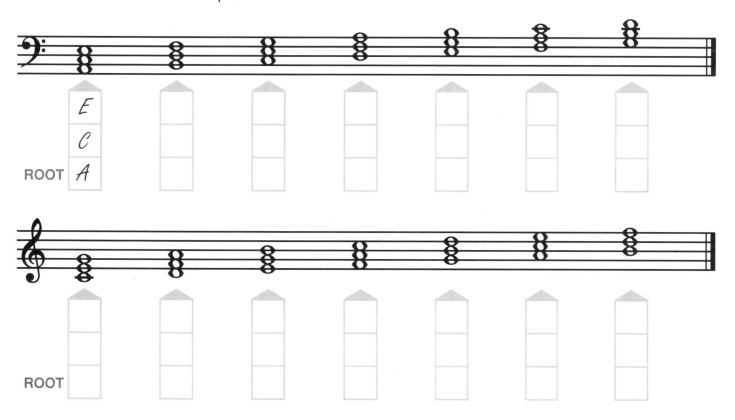

2. Fill in the blank squares with the missing note of each triad, as shown in the first example.

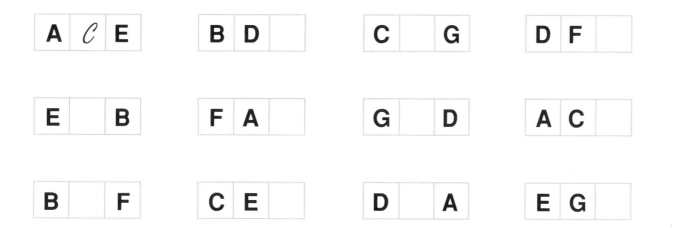

CHECK: Have you skipped one letter of the musical alphabet between the notes of every triad on this page?

Use with pages 14–15.

Triad Puzzle

If you know your TRIAD VOCABULARY, this puzzle can be solved very quickly.

If you do NOT know it, this puzzle will help you learn it.

Fill in the puzzle with TRIADS, using the given letter name as the ROOT.

If you make a mistake you will soon know it, because the puzzle will not work!

ACROSS

3. A	11. C	20. G
4. F	13. D	21. E
6. G	14. B	22. D
9. F	15. G	24. E
10. D	17. A	25. C

DOWN

1. F	8. D	18. C
2. C	12. G	19. E
4. F	13. D	23. A
5. A	15. G	24. E
7. B	16. B	

Use with the TOP HALF of page 16.

The Primary Triads

The PRIMARY TRIADS of any key are built on the 1st, 4th, & 5th notes of the scale.

The chords are identified by the Roman numerals **I**, **IV**, & **V** (1, 4, & 5).

In the key of C: The **I** CHORD (1 chord) is the C TRIAD.
　　　　　　　The **IV** CHORD (4 chord) is the F TRIAD.
　　　　　　　The **V** CHORD (5 chord) is the G TRIAD.

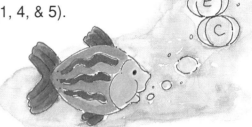

The PRIMARY TRIADS IN C MAJOR in the bass clef:

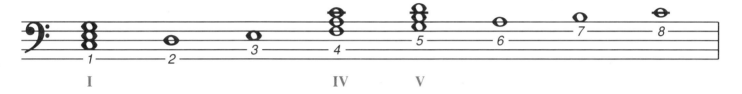

1. Build the PRIMARY TRIADS IN C MAJOR in the treble clef.
   Add two notes to the 1st, 4th, & 5th notes of the scale to complete the triads.

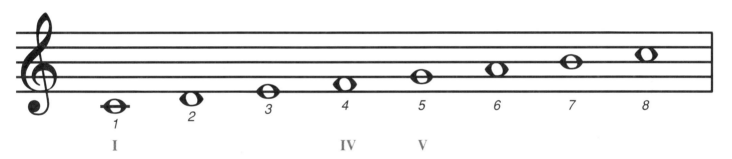

2. Write the ROMAN NUMERAL for each of these triads in the key of C MAJOR.

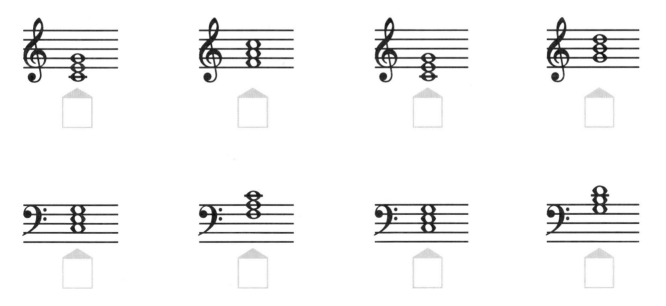

3. Play the above triads, saying the ROMAN NUMERAL of each as you play.
   Use RH 1 3 5 for the triads in treble clef. Use LH 5 3 1 for the triads in bass clef.

Use with the BOTTOM HALF of page 16.

About Chord Progressions

When we change from one chord to another, we call this a CHORD PROGRESSION.
When all chords are in root position, the hand must LEAP from one chord to the next.

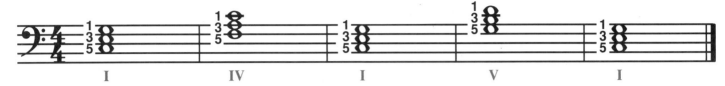

By using other positions for the **IV** and **V** chords, the same progression can be played more smoothly. Notice there is always *one* finger that does *not* have to move when the chords change!

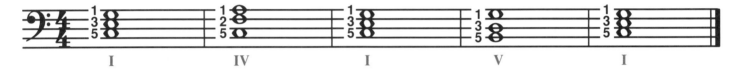

1. Play the above two lines. Notice that it is impossible to hold the notes of the first line for their full values. Which line makes the smoothest progression?

Rockin' Progression

2. Write the ROMAN NUMERALS in the boxes.
3. Play. The triads used in the RH are the same as those used in the LH.

Moderate rock tempo

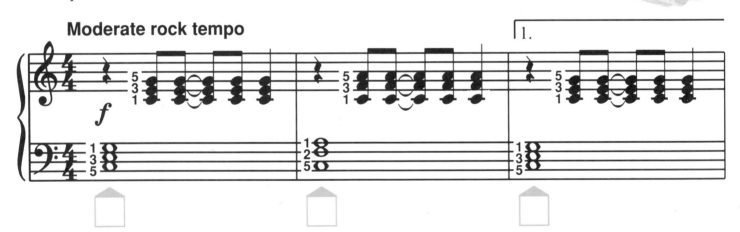

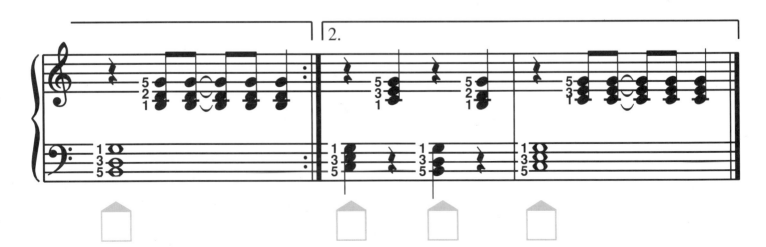

More About Triads

REMINDER:

When a triad is in **ROOT POSITION,**
the notes are stacked in 3rds,
touching one another like this:

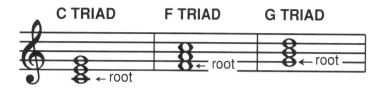

The ROOT is ALWAYS the LOWEST note!

The POSITION of a triad may be changed by moving one or more of its notes up or down an octave. Because of this, the root is sometimes NOT on the bottom but it is still easy to find!

When a triad is NOT in root position, there is always an interval of a 4th, leaving a gap like this:

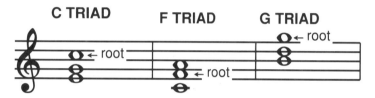

The ROOT is ALWAYS the note just above the gap!

1. Draw an arrow (←———) pointing to the ROOT of each triad, as shown in the first example.
2. Write the name of each triad in the upper boxes.
3. Write the ROMAN NUMERAL each triad would have in the key of C MAJOR in the lower boxes.

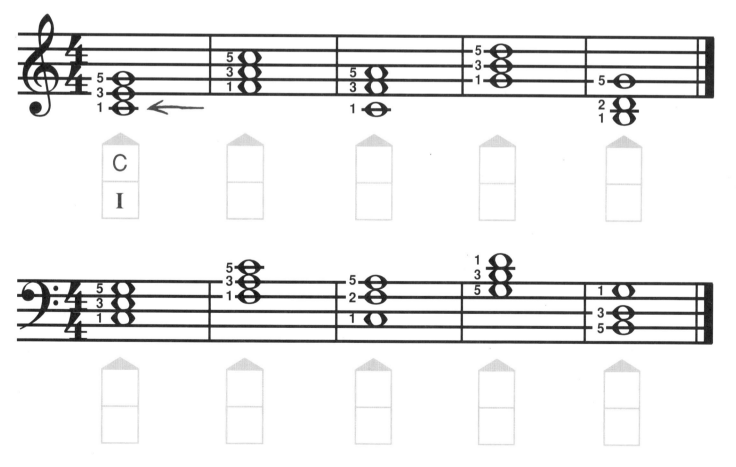

4. Play all of the above triads.

The I & V7 Chords in C Major

Use with page 18.

You have already played the **I** and **V** TRIADS in C MAJOR.

In most music, a **V7** chord is used instead of a **V** triad.

To make a 7th CHORD, a note an interval of a 7th above the root is added to a TRIAD.

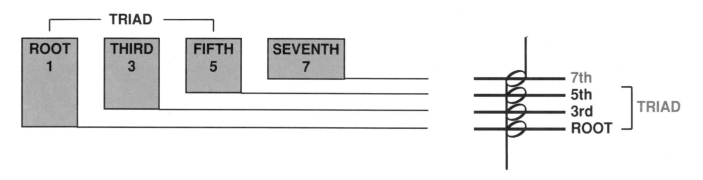

V7 built on the 5th note of the C SCALE:

For smooth and easy progressions:
• The 5th (D) is omitted.
• The 3rd (B) and 7th (F) are moved down an octav

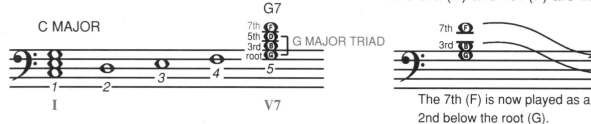

The 7th (F) is now played as a 2nd below the root (G).

The I–V7 Progression in C Major

1. Play the following several times.

LH 1 plays G in both chords.

RH 5 plays G in both chords.

Rockin' with V7

2. Write the ROMAN NUMERALS in the boxes.
3. Play. Notice how the triads in the RH agree with those in the LH.

Moderate rock tempo

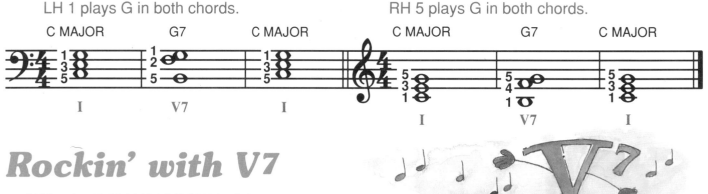

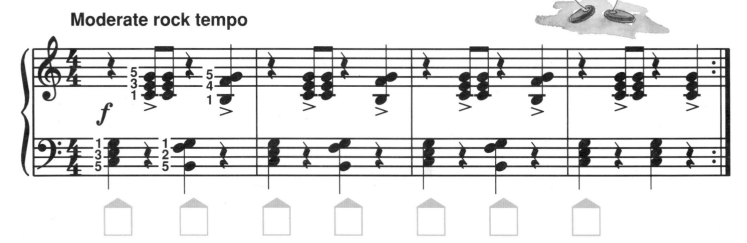

More About the I–V⁷ Progression in C Major

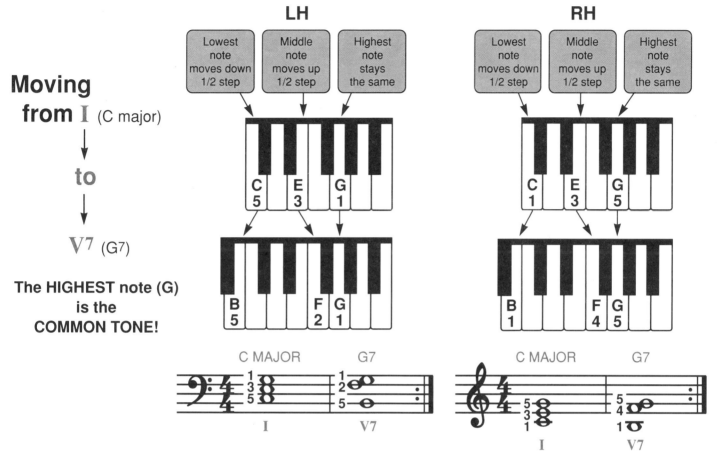

Moving from I (C major)

↓

to

↓

V⁷ (G7)

The HIGHEST note (G) is the COMMON TONE!

1. Practice changing from the C MAJOR chord to G7 as shown above, first with the LH, then with the RH. **REMEMBER:** The common tone (G) is played by the same finger in both chords.
2. Write the NAMES of the chords (C or G7) in the wide boxes ABOVE each of the following staffs.
3. Write the correct ROMAN NUMERALS (I or V7) in the square boxes BELOW each of the following staffs.
4. Play twice, first saying the chord names, and then saying the Roman numerals ("one chord" or "five-seven chord").

Use with page 20.

The Primary Chords in C Major

You have learned that the three PRIMARY TRIADS in the key of C major are the C TRIAD (**I**), the F TRIAD (**IV**) and the G TRIAD (**V**).

When we use the **V7** CHORD instead of the **V** TRIAD, we speak of the three PRIMARY CHORDS in C major. These are:

These positions are used for smooth progressions:

The Primary Chords in C Major

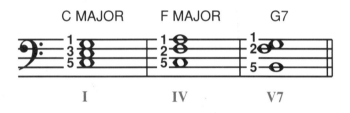

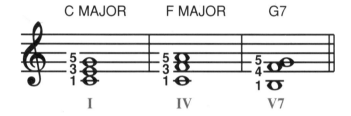

1. Write the PRIMARY CHORDS in C MAJOR, using the above positions.
2. Play. Say "One chord, four chord, five-seven chord" as you play.

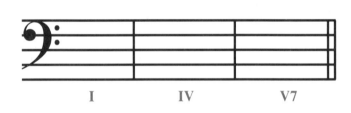

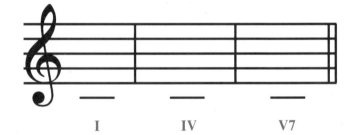

Rockin' with I, IV & V7

3. Write the ROMAN NUMERALS in the boxes, then play.

Moderate rock tempo

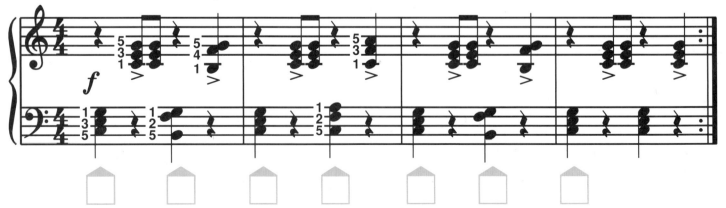

More About the I–IV Progression in C Major

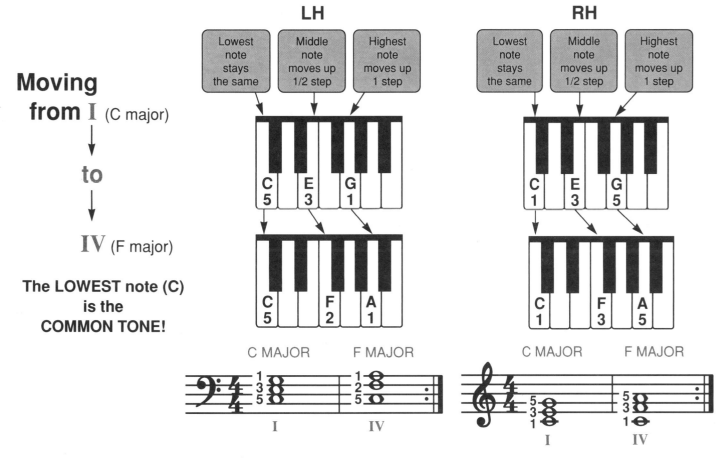

Moving from I (C major)

↓

to

↓

IV (F major)

The LOWEST note (C) is the COMMON TONE!

1. Practice changing from the C MAJOR to the F MAJOR chord as shown above, first with the LH, then with the RH. **REMEMBER:** The common tone (C) is played by the same finger in both chords.

2. Write the NAMES of the chords (C, F or G7) in the wide boxes ABOVE each of the following staffs.

3. Write the correct ROMAN NUMERALS (**I**, **IV** or **V7**) in the square boxes BELOW each of the following staffs.

4. Play twice, first saying the chord names, and then saying the Roman numerals ("one chord," "four chord" or "five-seven chord").

Use with pages 22–23.

Identifying 7th Chords

In this book you will be playing three different 7th chords. They will be very easy to recognize.

When the 7th chord is not in root position,
it always contains an interval of a 2nd.

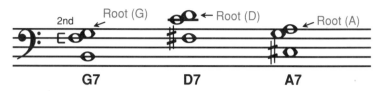

The ROOT is ALWAYS the upper note of the 2nd!

1. Draw an arrow (◄———) pointing to the ROOT of each 7th chord.
2. Write the name of each chord in the box below it.
   The CHORD NAME is the same as the ROOT NAME.

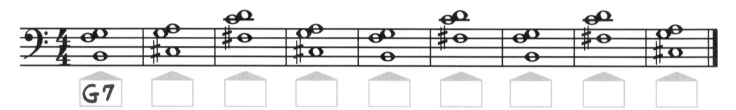

Chord Quiz (Review)

3. If you are not certain how to identify the root of a TRIAD
   in all positions, review page 11 of this book.
   If you are not certain how to identify a 7th chord
   in all positions, review the top of this page.
4. Draw an arrow (◄———) pointing to the ROOT
   of each of the following chords.
5. Write the name of each chord in the box below it.

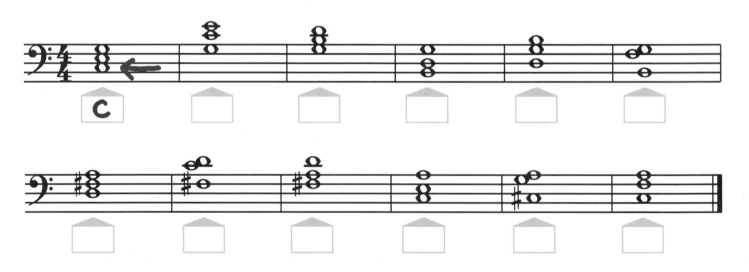

6. How many of the above chords are 7th chords?   ANSWER _____

Score 5 for each correct answer on this page.

PERFECT SCORE = 100   YOUR SCORE _____

Block Chords and Broken Chords

When ALL the notes of a chord are played TOGETHER, it is called a BLOCK CHORD.

When the notes of a chord are played ONE AT A TIME, it is called a BROKEN CHORD.

BLOCK CHORDS IN C MAJOR

 **I** Chord (C major)

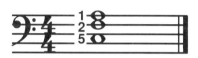 **IV** Chord (F major)

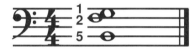 **V**⁷ Chord (G⁷)

BROKEN CHORDS IN C MAJOR

1. In the UPPER BASS STAFF of the music below, write the correct BLOCK CHORD, as indicated by the Roman numerals.
2. In the LOWER BASS STAFF, write BROKEN CHORDS, using the pattern given in the first measure.

3. Play, using BLOCK CHORDS in the LH.
4. Play, using BROKEN CHORDS in the LH.

Use with page 26.

The I & V⁷ Chords in G Major

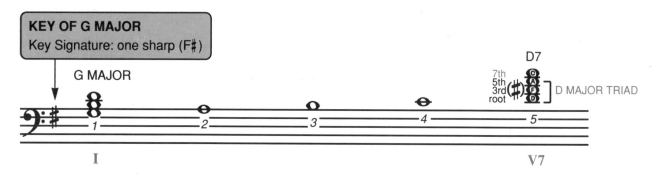

KEY OF G MAJOR
Key Signature: one sharp (F♯)

G MAJOR

D7

D MAJOR TRIAD

I

V7

For a smoother and easier progression, the D⁷ chord
is moved to a lower position and the 5th (A) is omitted.

G MAJOR

D7

I

V7

The I–V⁷ Progression in G Major

1. Play the following several times.

LH 1 plays D in both chords.

RH 5 plays D in both chords.

G MAJOR   D7   G MAJOR   G MAJOR   D7   G MAJOR

I   V7   I   I   V7   I

Study in G

WITH BLOCK AND BROKEN CHORDS

2. Write the names of the chords in the boxes above the staff.
3. Write the Roman numerals in the boxes below the staff.
4. Play twice, first saying the chord names, then saying the Roman numerals.

Moderato

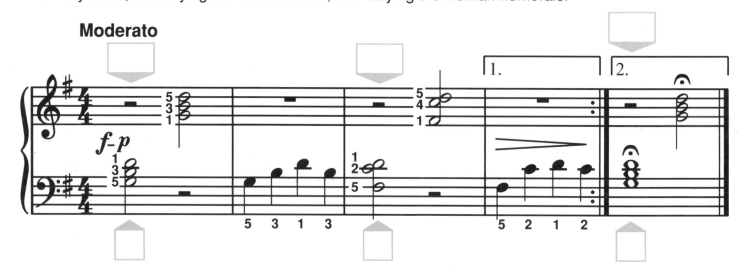

More About the I–V⁷ Progression in G Major

Moving from I (G major)

↓

to

↓

V⁷ (D7)

The HIGHEST note (D) is the COMMON TONE!

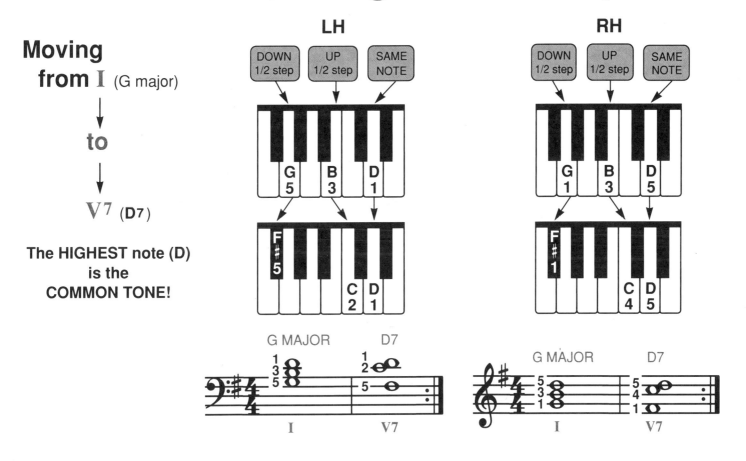

1. Practice changing from the G MAJOR to the D⁷ chord as shown above, first with the LH,
   then with the RH. **REMEMBER:** The common tone (D) is played by the same finger in both chords.

Broken Chords in ¾ Time

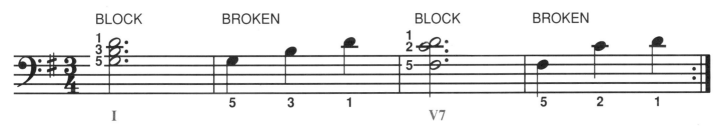

2. Write the Roman numerals of the broken chords in the boxes below the staff.
3. Play.

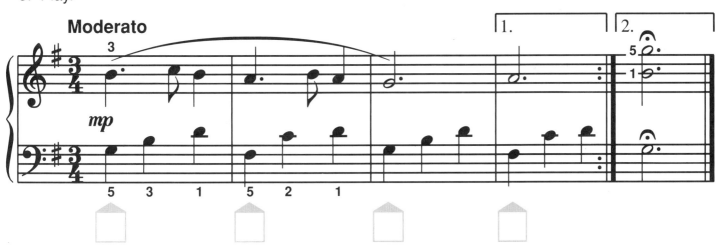

Use with page 28.

The Primary Chords in G Major

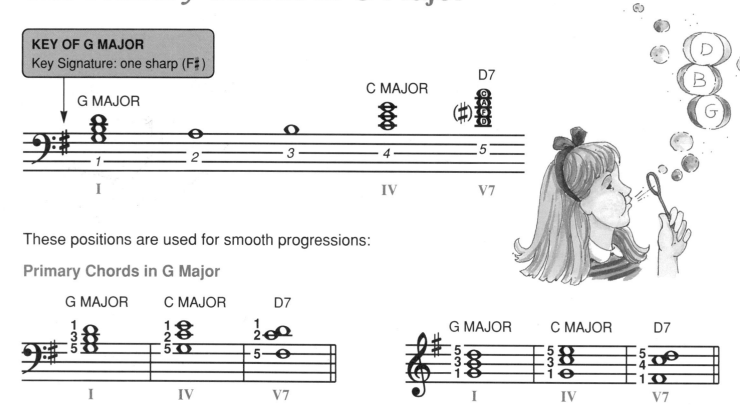

KEY OF G MAJOR
Key Signature: one sharp (F♯)

G MAJOR

C MAJOR

D7

I   IV   V7

These positions are used for smooth progressions:

Primary Chords in G Major

G MAJOR   C MAJOR   D7

I   IV   V7

G MAJOR   C MAJOR   D7

I   IV   V7

1. Add the G MAJOR key signature to each staff below.
2. Write the PRIMARY CHORDS in the KEY OF G MAJOR, using the above positions.

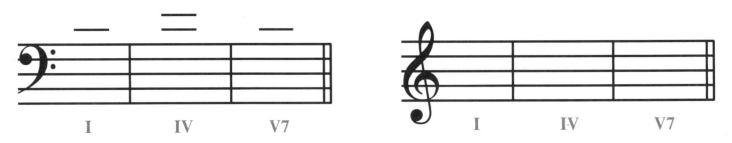

I   IV   V7

I   IV   V7

3. Write the ROMAN NUMERALS (**I**, **IV**, or **V7**) in the boxes.
4. Play.

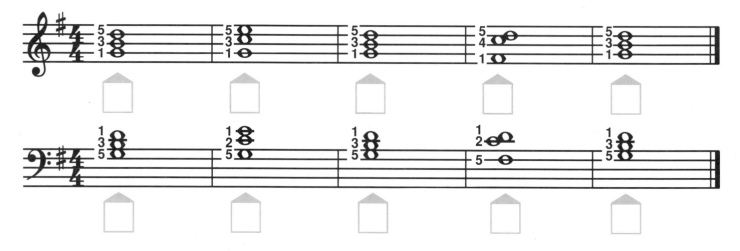

5. OPTIONAL: Play hands together.

More About the I–IV Progression in G Major

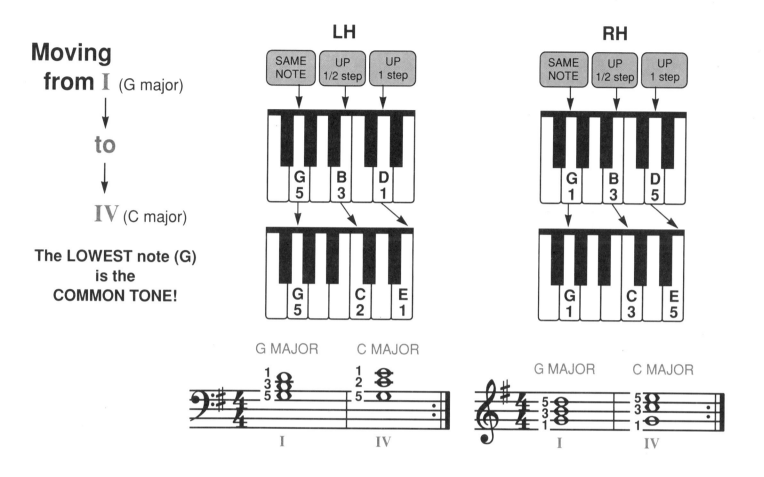

**Moving
from I** (G major)

to

IV (C major)

The LOWEST note (G)
is the
COMMON TONE!

1. Practice changing from the G MAJOR to the C MAJOR CHORD as shown above, first with the LH, then with the RH. **REMEMBER:** The common tone (G) is played by the same finger in both chords.

2. Write the names of the chords (G, C or D^7) in the boxes above the staffs.
3. Write the Roman numerals (**I**, **IV**, or **V 7**) in the boxes below the staffs.
4. Play each line twice, first saying the chord names, then saying the Roman numerals.

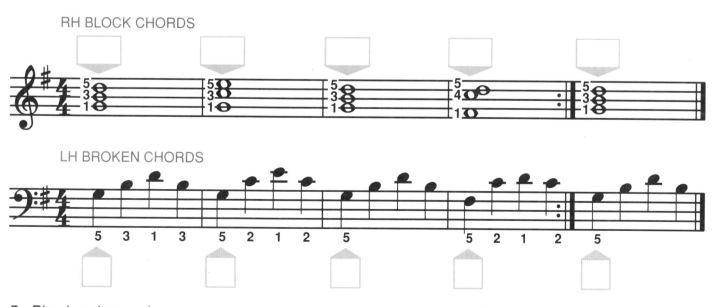

RH BLOCK CHORDS

LH BROKEN CHORDS

5. Play hands together.

Use with pages 32–33.

Crossing 3 over 1
to play the D Major Scale

1. Write the letter names of the notes of the D MAJOR SCALE, from *left* to *right,* on the keyboard below. Be sure the WHOLE STEPS and HALF STEPS are correct!

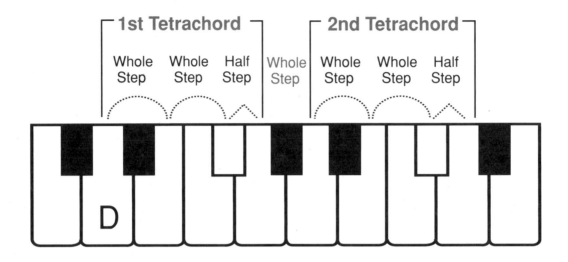

2. Complete the tetrachord beginning on D. Write one note over each finger number.

3. Complete the tetrachord beginning on A. Write one note over each finger number.

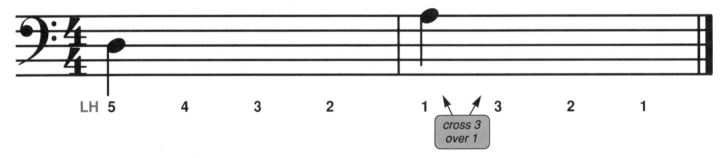

THIS IS THE COMPLETE D MAJOR SCALE, ASCENDING.

4. Play the D major scale with the LH, crossing 3 over 1.

5. Write the finger numbers over the notes of the following scale, starting with 5 and crossing 3 over 1.

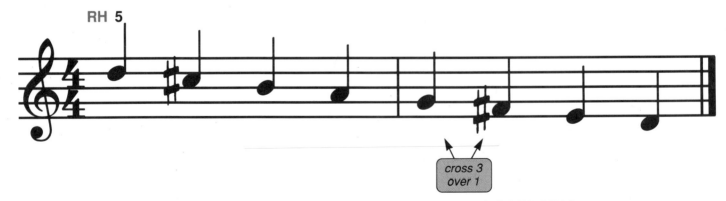

THIS IS THE COMPLETE D MAJOR SCALE, DESCENDING.

6. Play the D major scale with the RH, crossing 3 over 1.

The I & V⁷ Chords in D Major

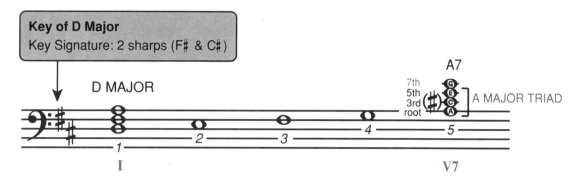

For a smoother and easier progression, the A⁷ chord
is moved to a lower position and the 5th (E) is omitted.

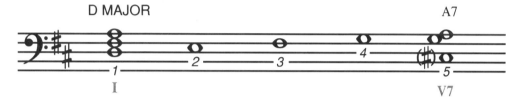

The I–V⁷ Progression in D Major

1. Play the following several times.

LH 1 plays A in both chords.   RH 5 plays A in both chords.

Study in D

WITH BLOCK AND BROKEN CHORDS

2. Write the names of the chords in the boxes
   above the staff.
3. Write the Roman numerals in the boxes
   below the staff.
4. Play twice, first saying the chord names, then saying
   the Roman numerals.

Moderato

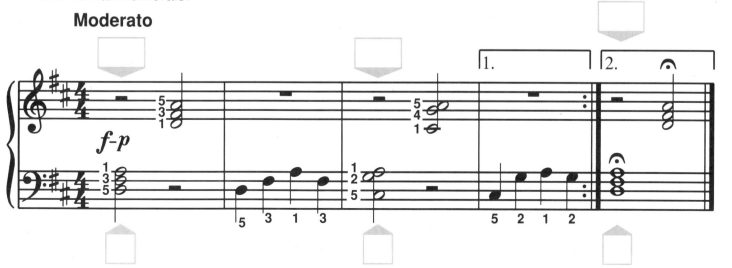

Use with page 35.

More About the I–V⁷ Progression in D Major

Moving from I (D major)

↓

to

↓

V⁷ (A7)

The HIGHEST note (A) is the COMMON TONE!

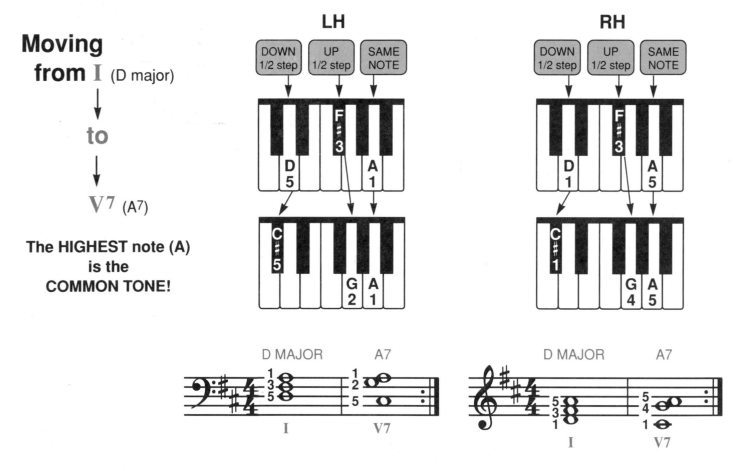

1. Practice changing from the D MAJOR to the A7 chord, as shown above, first with the LH, then with the RH. **REMEMBER:** The common tone (A) is played by the same finger in both chords.

Syncopated Tune in D

2. Write the Roman numerals of the broken chords in the boxes below the staff.

3. Play.

Allegro moderato

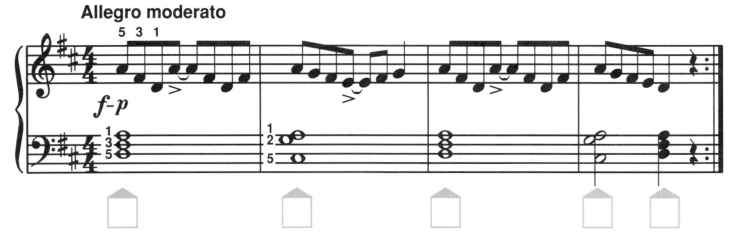

The Primary Chords in D Major

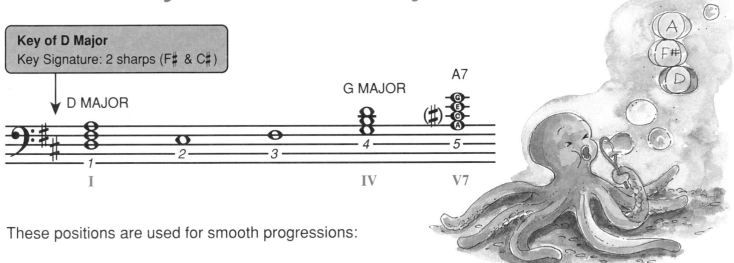

Key of D Major
Key Signature: 2 sharps (F♯ & C♯)

D MAJOR   G MAJOR   A7

These positions are used for smooth progressions:

Primary Chords in D Major

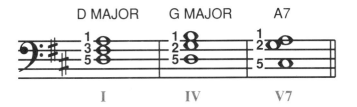

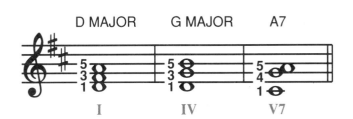

1. Add the D MAJOR key signature to each staff below.
2. Write the PRIMARY CHORDS in the KEY OF D MAJOR, using the above positions.

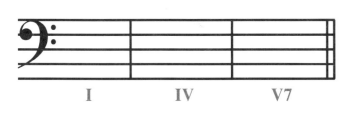

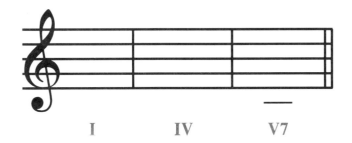

3. Write the ROMAN NUMERALS (**I**, **IV**, or **V7**) in the boxes.
4. Play.

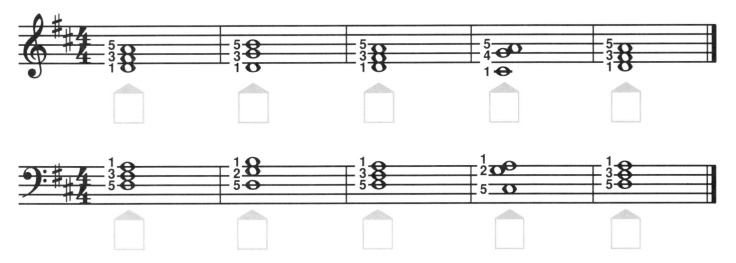

5. OPTIONAL: Play hands together.

Use with page 37.

More About the I–IV Progression in D Major

Moving from I (D major)

↓

to

↓

IV (G major)

The LOWEST note (D) is the COMMON TONE!

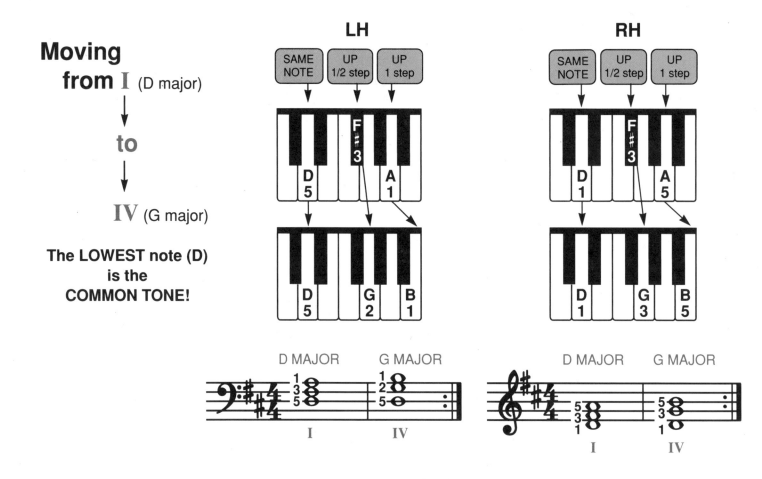

1. Practice changing from the D MAJOR to the G MAJOR CHORD as shown above, first with the LH, then with the RH. **REMEMBER:** The common tone (D) is played by the same finger in both chords.

2. Write the names of the chords (D, G or A7) in the boxes above the staffs.
3. Write the Roman numerals (**I**, **IV**, or **V7**) in the boxes below the staffs.
4. Play twice, first saying the chord names, then saying the Roman numerals.

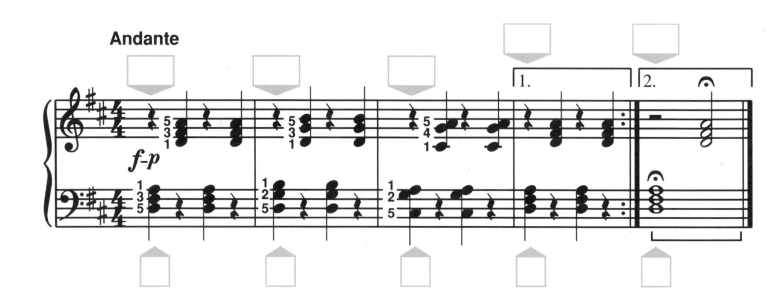

New Ways of Playing Broken Chords

Use the TOP HALF of this page with pages 38–39.

"Alberti Bass" in $\frac{2}{4}$ Time

The Italian composer, Domenico Alberti (1710–1740), used this type of bass in his keyboard compositions so frequently that it was named for him. It was also used by Haydn, Mozart, Beethoven and other great composers. It consists of chord tones played in this order: lowest, highest, middle, highest.

1. Write the chord names (D, G, A7) in the boxes above the staffs.
2. Write the Roman numerals (**I**, **IV**, or **V7**) in the boxes below the staffs.
3. Play the top line, then play the bottom line several times, slowly at first, gradually increasing speed to *Allegro.*

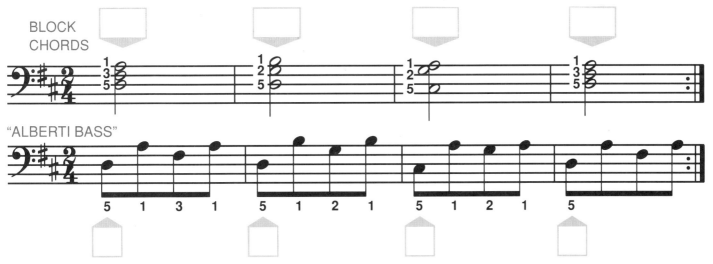

Use the BOTTOM HALF of this page with pages 40–41.

"Bass-Chord" Style

This popular style of accompaniment consists of the lowest chord note followed by the middle and highest notes played together as a two-note chord. In the following examples, the bottom line has the rhythm you will use in playing *O SOLE MIO* in the Lesson Book.

1. Write the chord names in the boxes above the staffs.
2. Write the Roman numerals in the boxes below the staffs.
3. Play the top line, then play the bottom two lines several times.

Use with pages 42–43.

The Big Puzzle

When you complete this *BIG PUZZLE* and pass *THE BIG QUIZ* on pages 30–31, plus *SCRAMBLED PRIMARIES* on page 32, you will be ready for promotion to Alfred's Basic Piano Course, Level 3. The clues for this puzzle are on the next page.

Score 3 points for each word correctly placed in the puzzle.

PERFECT SCORE = 120   YOUR SCORE _____

Clues for the Big Puzzle

ACROSS

2. Sign meaning "hold the note longer than its value."
4. Lines of the bass staff.
7. A sharp or flat not given in the key signature.
9. Italian word meaning "loud."
13. Italian word meaning "very soft."
16. The notes of a G tetrachord.
17. Italian word meaning "very loud."
19. The notes of an A TRIAD.
21. Two Italian words, meaning "moderately soft."
23. Notes of a G TRIAD.
24. Italian word meaning "rate of speed."
25. Notes of a D TRIAD.
28. Notes of an F TRIAD.
31. Four notes in alphabetical order, having the pattern of WHOLE STEP, WHOLE STEP, HALF STEP.
32. The first four notes of the musical alphabet.
35. $\frac{2}{4}, \frac{3}{4}, \frac{4}{4}$ These are: (two words).
37. Repeat from the beginning and play to the *Fine*. (Two letters and two words.)
38. Italian word meaning "smoothly connected."
39. This sign lowers a note a half step.

DOWN

1. Repeat from the beginning. (Two words.)
3. Italian word for "gradually slower." (Abbreviation.)
5. Notes of the B TRIAD.
6. Notes of the C TRIAD.
8. Sign showing how loud or soft to play. (Two words.)
10. The same bass pattern played over and over.
11. A piece to be sung.
12. Played ahead of the main beats and tied over.
14. This sign gives a note special emphasis.
15. Chords built on the 1st, 4th & 5th notes of the scale.
17. An interval that skips three white keys.
18. Two Italian words meaning "moderately loud."
20. An added ending.
22. A triad is a three note _ _ _ _ _.
26. The music between two bar lines.
27. A three note chord is a _ _ _ _ _.
29. The spaces of the bass staff.
30. This sign cancels a sharp or flat.
33. The notes of a C tetrachord.
34. The spaces of the treble staff.
36. A piece you play alone.

Words used in Puzzle

A B C D	DA CAPO	FORTISSIMO	PIANISSIMO
ACCENT	D.C. AL FINE	G A B C	PRIMARY
ACCIDENTAL	D F A	G B D	RIT.
A C E	DYNAMIC SIGN	G B D F A	SOLO
A C E G	F A C	LEGATO	SONG
B D F	F A C E	MEASURE	SYNCOPATED
C D E F	FERMATA	MEZZO FORTE	TEMPO
C E G	FIFTH	MEZZO PIANO	TETRACHORD
CHORD	FLAT	NATURAL	TIME SIGNATURES
CODA	FORTE	OSTINATO	TRIAD

Use with pages 44–45.

The Big Quiz

This NIFTY-FIFTY TRUE-FALSE QUIZ is your next landmark on the way to Level 3.
In the boxes, write T for TRUE, F for FALSE.

1. *BASSO OSTINATO* is a mistake made over and over in the bass.

2. *BASSO OSTINATO* is a pattern of notes played over and over in the bass.

3. *SYNCOPATED NOTES* are played exactly on the main beats of the measure.

4. *SYNCOPATED NOTES* are played between the main beats of the measure and held over.

5. *D.C. al Fine* means repeat the entire piece.

6. *D.C. al Fine* means repeat from the beginning, and end at the word *Fine*.

7. A *TRIAD* is a three-legged camera holder.

8. A *TRIAD* is a three-note chord.

9. The notes of a *G TRIAD* are G A B.

10. The notes of a *G TRIAD* are G B D.

11. The *PRIMARY CHORDS* in any key are the **I, IV, & V**⁷ chords.

12. The **V**⁷ chord is built on the 5th note of the scale.

13. A *FERMATA* indicates that a note should be held longer than its true value.

14. This is a *FERMATA:*

15. This is a *FERMATA:*

16. An *ACCIDENTAL* is a mistake.

17. An *ACCIDENTAL* is a sharp or flat that is not in the key signature.

18. This is an *ACCENT SIGN:*

19. This is an *ACCENT SIGN:* >

20. *Adagio, andante* and *allegro* are *DYNAMIC SIGNS.*

21. *Adagio, andante* and *allegro* are *TEMPO MARKS.*

22. *TEMPO* means time signature.

23. *TEMPO* means rate of speed.

24. A *CODA* is an added ending.

25. *ff* means fast and furious.

26. *ff* means very loud.

27. This sign means gradually louder.

28. *Fine* means you played well.

29. *Fine* means *THE END.*

30. *mp* means mighty pretty.

31. *mp* means moderately soft.

32. *mf* is softer than *mp.*

33. *pp* means play the piano.

34. *pp* means very soft.

35. A *SCALE* is the same as a *TETRACHORD.*

36. A *MAJOR SCALE* contains two *TETRACHORDS.*

37. $\frac{2}{4}, \frac{3}{4}, \frac{4}{4}$ are *KEY SIGNATURES.*

38. $\frac{2}{4}, \frac{3}{4}, \frac{4}{4}$ are *TIME SIGNATURES.*

39. *RITARDANDO* means gradually faster.

40. *RITARDANDO* means gradually slowing.

41. A *NATURAL SIGN* cancels a sharp or flat.

42. Two notes played separately make a *HARMONIC INTERVAL.*

43. The root of this chord is C:

44. The root of this chord is C:

45. The root of this chord is C:

46. The *KEY SIGNATURE* of the *KEY OF G MAJOR* is *1* sharp (F♯).

47. The *KEY SIGNATURE* of the *KEY OF D MAJOR* is 2 sharps (F♯ & C♯).

48. The *KEY SIGNATURE* of the *KEY OF C MAJOR* is *NO* sharps or flats.

49. When the notes of a chord are played one at a time, it is a *BLOCK CHORD.*

50. When the notes of a chord are played one at a time, it is a *BROKEN CHORD.*

Score 2 points for each correct answer.

PERFECT SCORE = 100   YOUR SCORE _____

Use with page 46.

Scrambled Primaries

In the boxes at the TOP of the page, the PRIMARY CHORDS in C, G & D major are given,
but they are not in any specific order.

On the BLANK STAFFS in the boxes at the bottom of the page,
write the same chords in the correct order.

I chords	IV chords	V7 chords

	I chords	IV chords	V7 chords
C Major			
G Major			
D Major			

Score 10 points for each correct chord, plus a 10 point bonus for finishing the book.

PERFECT SCORE = 100   YOUR SCORE _____